Much Possessed

Acknowledgements

Thanks are due to the following publications in which these poems have appeared: *Clear Poetry, The Interpreters House, The North, Running Out of Space, The Poetry Shed.*

'A City of the Plain', 'According to their Cloth', 'What the Owls Saw' and 'What the Owls Dreamed' were written as part of the Leads to Leeds project, led by Helen Mort and published on the website.

'Untrammelled' won 2nd Prize in The Havant Poetry Competition 2015. 'Milton's Daughter' was highly commended in the 2015 Manchester Cathedral Competition 2015. 'At Tarskavaig' won The Plough Poetry Competition 2014. 'Bheinn na Caillich' won The McLellan Competion 2015. 'True Naming' was highly commended in the Charles Causley Foundation Competition 2015. 'Banked Up' won second prize in the Ilkley Literature Festival Competition 2014 and 'Short back-and-sides' won the Ilkley Literature Festival Competition 2015. 'A Proper Job' won second prize in The Poetry Business Yorkshire Prize 2015. 'A Cunning Woman' won The Red Shed Postcode Prize 2015.

Particular thanks to the organisers of, and tutors on, inspirational residential writing courses in St Ives, in Whitby, in Cumbria, in Rydal and in Alicante: to Christopher North and The Old Olive Press; to Kim Moore, Steve Ely, Carola Luther and Jane Draycott. To Clare Shaw and Kim Moore for reading my manuscript. To the regular writing days at Bank Street in Sheffield that keep me fuelled and fired; to all the poets I meet there, and to the Monday writers' workshops of the Albert Poets in Huddersfield. To my friends at The Puzzle Poets Live in Sowerby Bridge, and particularly to Bob Horne. To all organisers of poetry open mics, and especially to Keith Hutson. To my friend and former pupil, Andy Blackford. Above all to my partner Flo, for her insistence that I get stuff done.

Much Possessed
John Foggin

smith|doorstop

Published 2016 by
smith|doorstop books
The Poetry Business
Bank Street Arts
32-40 Bank Street
Sheffield S1 2DS
www.poetrybusiness.co.uk

Copyright © John Foggin 2016

ISBN 978-1-910367-63-6

John Foggin hereby asserts his moral right to be identified as the author of this book.

British Library Cataloguing-in-Publication Data.
A catalogue record for this book is available from the British Library.

Typeset by Utter
Printed and bound by CPI Group (UK) Ltd, Croydon, CR0 4YY

smith|doorstop is a member of Inpress, www.inpressbooks.co.uk. Distributed by Central Books Ltd., 99 Wallis Road, London E9 5LN.

The Poetry Business receives financial support from Arts Council England

Contents

- 9   A Story
- 11   Scrumping
- 12   While
- 13   Milton's Daughter goes to Market
- 14   The Priest and the Ploughman go Skating
- 15   What he said
- 16   It starts with a lie
- 17   At Tarskavaig
- 18   11, Achnacloich
- 19   Effie
- 20   Blended
- 21   Bheinn na Caillich
- 23   A Kind of History
- 25   Richard before Bosworth
- 26   A Pibroch for (MacCaig)
- 28   For the true naming of the world
- 29   In the Meantime
- 30   Much Possessed
- 31   Bounty
- 32   Wren
- 33   Goldcrest
- 34   Whether it cared or not
- 35   A Dry Place
- 36   Lacerta Lapida
- 37   One Sunday
- 39   Colouring in
- 40   First Pressing
- 42   All over the city
- 44   A City of the Plain

45	According to their Cloth
46	Short Back and Sides
48	What the Owls Saw
50	What the Owls Dreamed
52	A Proper Job
54	A Dreadful Trade
56	A Cunning Woman
57	Myra
58	Winnie
60	Banked up
61	Lutenist
62	Chimes
63	Cold Comfort
65	St Ives/ Porthmeor 1953
66	This much
67	I made this box
69	It was a morning like this
71	A Weak Force
73	Above all: Mallory on Everest
74	Untrammelled
76	Falling apart
78	Seen from Above
79	When the keel grated
80	The Fisherman's Church of Talmont-sur-Gironde
81	Curtain call

*For my three wise sisters, Hilary Elfick,
Gaia Holmes and Kim Moore*

A Story

Let me tell you about stories
Stories are real.
I'll tell you about the snake.

Innocent, in the way
of the simple, the uncomplicated.
Don't blame the snake,

who could never speak, its tongue
being a wonderful thing
for tasting the informative air.

Cold blooded, long-spined,
flexible, designed to lie
in the heat of the day

to fill himself with sun,
a quick dry thing, lovely
and tessellate.

What was the snake thinking?
Not a thing. But I,
Lucifer. Ah well.

A thing of light, hurled
headlong, the radiance
of heaven guttering in my breast

with no redress
no hope, no prospect
of remission or return.

God stole my name.
I'll have him kill his Son
I'll nail him to the Tree.

I'll have him bleed
I'll show him how the fruit
of Good and Evil tastes

and there shall be
no harrowing
nor Resurrection.

Believe me.
    Stories are real.

Scrumping

It wasn't the apples, small and sour;
God could just as well have said:

that one cat with the cool yellow eyes ...
that one you shall never ever stroke;

that turquoise fragile egg you will not take from the nest
between finger and thumb, hold it up to the light;

where the stream falls thirty feet in a tumble of white,
that round pool; there you may not dip a toe, however hot the day.

Well. How could you not?

The cat would scratch, the egg would smash,
the cold of the pool would stop your heart.

But first it would race and buzz, and after all
why would God make you that way, wind you up

and let you go, unless he just wanted to make sure
that was the way you worked. And you did.

While

the Angel Raphael and Adam debated
a heliocentric universe, the problems
with the maths of epicycles, Eve gave a twist
to the apple and, in the fashion of apples,
it fell right into her hand. She tested
its ripeness with the soft pad of a thumb,
the give of its skin with a crescent of nail,
its wet white flesh with her perfect teeth,
and its acid sweetness filled the dark
of her soft mouth like a cushioned pearl,
till her palate and tongue thought they knew
the apple inside out, and sang songs
of sweetness. The acid just bided its time,
slowly dissolving the pearl till nothing
was left but the dark at the core, slaked ash
and the dull grey ghost of the pearl.
The sun went on shining, the earth kept turning,
the angel and Adam never noticed a thing.

Milton's Daughter goes to Market

Always I leave the house and think
how good it would be not to come back.
Or, return and find it other.
All the shutters open.
And yes, I know they are.
But in a house of the blind
they may as well be barred.

To return to good absences,
to no close smell of fustian black,
no odour of wax, or ink, or the singe of a feather,
no scrape of pewter, scratch of vellum,
no toneless rise and fall of angels, seraphim,
of darkness visible, rhetoric,
grandiloquence, the huge illimitable
exhausting suffocating universe.

How good to return to a room
brimming with no Lucifer,
no Eve, no Adam,
no fruit, no Fall,
but simple things.
Like bread. A bowl of milk. Apples.

The Priest and the Ploughman go Skating

Hard and slippery, there's no purchase,
unless, for one, a consolation of a kind in bleakness,
the indifference of God, his chill disciplines
and the fear of falling, the nothing of stilled water
and the darkness under all,
and for the other
the thought of earthfasts rising in his frozen fields,
a broken ploughshare
and a shrunk clamp of beets in the lee of a barn.

They have no language for not working.
They want for the cold flags of a chapel,
a plain altar, absolution
for what will not be, precisely, named;
or
just a dusting of snow, the red of the Fordson,
sharp blue exhaust, a clutter of gulls
and a straight furrow.

What he said

In my cupped palm
I would have held you
like a shell
close to my ear
and singing drowned
deep in your ebb your flow
your swell

It starts with a lie

and where else would it start
only with one who said that he
would walk for me see for me breathe
for me love me and that was a lie
that I lived as my lashes grew long
my arms shrank to my sides
I could not hold a comb
had no need of a comb
becoming a shape no more
I could not take a step
being helpless being just a shape
till the rain and the big wind and the tide
made me light
and water was natural to me
in its depths and its turns
and I called him to join me
and I called so quiet
I thought that he might not
hear in the wind and the surge of the sea
but he thought he could change
but he said he would change
stepping out of his clothes
and he truly believed
I believe and he ran in the sea and he drowned
and now am I where
there is no cold and no lies
but the balancing round of the ocean
and now I can sleep

At Tarskavaig

Washed up on a rucked-rug shoreline
with floats, fish-boxes, trawlermen's gloves,
fertiliser sacks, kelp, clots of wool,
the cockle-pickers. Peat-cured, with ruined teeth,
long, dirty nails, eyes as dark as iodine.

They tinkers. Och. says Effie. You'd do well
look to the barns, and count the spades,
and what did they ask you for?

Those women, old coats belted with rope,
rubber boots patched with gaffer tape,
hair like seaweed, when they tapped
on the windscreen, brown as selkies?

For a light only, the bright ember,
blue smoke blown on the wind, the spit
of rain off the sea, and thanks we're away
down the road and done with the day,
with turning stones, and bladderwrack,
browsing the cold shore for cockles,
to fill a knuckly net ... iron, amber, cobalt, rust.

What's to be done with Tarskavaig tinkers
who come up out of the peat or the sea?
And when the light goes, where do they turn?

11, Achnacloich

a flicker of white water on the burn
below the alders where the heron roosts

a flirt of dunnock in the short grass
that sets the sheep trotting

rain dragging its skirts
across the skerries in the ebb

right on the rim of the moor
three hinds, watching

A curl of bluegrey turf smoke
from the red-roofed croft

This is how it stays

The heron just crumpling
into the alders,
like a broken kite
the deer watching
between the moor and the sky
small birds lifting from the field
like the hem of a skirt in a breeze
the lamentations of sheep
the bright red tin roof of a crofter's house

Effie

eats her slice of cake with care,
pinches up its crumbs,
always leaves her boots outside.
She'll not have cheese with fruit cake;
she's too polite to say so,
but knows it isn't right.

She misses him smoking behind the barn
as if he thought she wouldn't know.

She saw an otter just last week,
with two young ones, playing
where the burn runs into the sea.
She smiles.

That dog he drove all the way
to Tyndrum to buy is daft; and, yes,
it takes no notice. It stops and starts.
The sheep run anyhow.
Och. Well. Thank you for the cake.

One year, she came up to the house,
November, midnight almost,
to make sure we'd not miss
the shimmer of smoke and silver
above the Cuillin, the whole sky
strangely light and shivering
like the sea.

Blended

That would be the time I saw the White-tailed eagle,
the time Norman says Well, yes, I'll take another,
the time he came up to the cottage, which is a thing
he rarely does; it would be Effie, usually,
who'd have a cup of tea, a slice of Dundee cake,
but Norman says cake's not his thing, and coughs,
thoughtfully, because sheep dip will do that
over the years, it'll get to the lungs, so then
we settle on the whisky; not a single malt –
the Isle of Skye that's blended in the South,
in pawky Edinburgh, but like Angus
at the Post Office by the ferry always says:
it's a wee bit smoky-peaty, and och it's no
to everybody's taste, but it turns out
it tastes just fine, which is how it comes to be
that Norman takes a generous third glass
and spreads himself a little and says
that last year, driving back from Armadale,
just where the road comes over the moor
above Loch Dughail, just before it twists
down the three miles through the birches,
just there, and was it June? Och, summer, anyway
and right there above the loch, and it was a day
so still, there was a White-tailed eagle, sailing
in off Slapin, and not a wingbeat to it now,
and there it was, and there it was reflected
in the loch, and you know, that was a lovely thing,
the eagle in the wind and on the water.
And I know that though I never saw the eagle
ride the wind to Rhum, I know I saw it then
with Norman, comfy in the armchair,
with that third glass of smoky-peaty
blended Isle of Skye.

Bheinn na Caillich

Because they had the mastery of iron,
because the land was thin and hard,
because the sea was the way to everything,
because nothing could gainsay
a well-caulked, lapstraked boat
with a flare at the bow that perfectly
fit a space the water would make for it,
because their oceans were swanspaths, whaleroads.
because they wrote their maps in the wind,
in the run of the cod, of the herring, of the cloud,
the way the gulls would go; because of that

they sailed out from granite fjords;
cargoed with amber and jet and beaver pelts,
red river gold and wolfskins;
over the Dogger, the mouth of the Rhine,
round Cape Wrath, to the Irish Sea, Biscay,
the gates of the Mediterranean,
its hot shores, its painted boats
and whitesailed dhows as bright as ghosts,
and all for the lapis, amethysts, white gold
they spun into knotwork dragons swallowing their tails;
bracelets, cloakpins, breastpins, clasps and rings.

Who counted the hours of tillage,
the scantlings of barley and oats,
the frozen sleet on longship shrouds,
skin torn on intractable nets,
or how many million herring and cod
shrank in the wind on racks of spruce?

Who told how it was
after all the work of hands and years,
they could fashion chests of black bog-oak,
bind them with ironstrips ,
lock up the lapis, the gold, the bright enamels
and bury them high in the eye of the wind
on a red granite summit over snowfield and scree
in a grave with a princess anointed and shrouded,
how they might raise a great cairn,
with chockstone and boulder,
and no one would touch it.

A Kind of History

> *Glencoe has no melancholy except that which men bring to it,
> remembering history*
>   – John Prebble

MacIan of MacDonald of Glencoe
comes to Inverary; three bitter days
of blizzard at year's ending;
three days from the Fords of Ballachulish,
the Narrows of Creran by Benderloch,
the Pass of Brander below Bheinn Cruachan;
by Loch Fyne and Glen Aray to the sea.

In sodden plaid, and blind with snow,
his oath denied, Macdonald of Glencoe is weeping.
History does not tell what for.

At the Falls of Glencoe lay-by, these days
the piper jingles coins in his bonnet;
skirls Flower of Scotland for the one in ten
hacked and harried in the reek
of each small house, and for the rest
shrinking into the snowy night of the Glen
where contour lines are packed like fingerprints,
where there is a name for every burn,
for every corrie, ridge and bealach.

Valley of Slate and Churn. Corrie of Capture.
Ridge of Eagles,
Aonach Eagach.
Sgurr na Fonnadh, Bheinn a Creachin, Achriachtan,

as though they staked their claim with a language
thistly with scratchy consonants.

When they fled through black snows
into a white dawn, half-dressed, unshod,
they melted into the screes
of high corries where they'd penned their rustled herds,
and everywhere they hid, they'd named and knew.

Who can say who they were.

Richard before Bosworth

Boy. There's no need for you to stay. I can fettle
all this gear. The rest have all fucked off.
Go if you've a mind. There's no one'll blame you.
I shan't. That priest made himself scarce,
the canting ingrate. But I tell you this. By God,
I stand here your rightful and anointed king.
Blessed by three suns rising in the smoking frost
the day that Edward died and the Lord did grant
to us the field. Bustle then. Make yourself useful.
Buckle on this shoulder brace. Pull this strap tight.
Don't look surprised. What did you expect?
A hump like a fucking minotaur? One wasted
leg, a lurching gait. Not quite the monster, then?
Never killed a man I wasn't looking in the eye.
That bastard Richmond and his traitor's lies ...
bottled spider that bitch Margaret calls me.
Listen. Your age I was riding chargers.
Those slick-tongued pretty boys. I'll tell you what.
I'll not burn in hell for that fat whoreson, Clarence.
Drowned in a butt of malmsey? The fuck he did.
Drank himself to death, god rot him. I had
their women? Course I did. And so would you
The Lady Anne? O yes. Spat right in my face.
I waited for a day or two. Don't look like that.
A sweet armful, Anne. Said I made her laugh.
More ways than one to skin a cat. Do I see ghosts?
Round every corner, boy. Kill enough, and so will you.
Don't think I lose a fucking minute's sleep.
All my family butchered. I can't smell blood these days.
Right. You've done a grand job with these greaves.
Light a candle for me if I don't come back.
Get yourself to York and light it there.
Give me my sword. By God's grace I am
England's king. So. Let us go to it. Pray for me.

A Pibroch for (MacCaig)

> *History frightens me ...*
> *If only I come to be a word with brackets round it,*
> *a word drowned in a footnote,*
> *a word*
>   – Norman MacCaig, 'Backward look', 1984

What was it he wrote about death?
'the one that smiles ruefully
thinking how little he is understood.'

MacCaig, punctilious as a dipper,
pertinent and spry as a robin
on the precise tips of his verse.
What a look he'd give me,
laconic, spare and handsome,
holding his cigarette like a matinee idol.

It's just that I come to him late
and he bothers me with death:
that cart on the shore road,
the one coming with the sack in his hand,
the scyther in the hayfield,
those blind horizons, black sails.

I keep wondering: why;
here, in this land of birds,
the generous skies of Assynt,
why these shadows, this shadow?

I should pay more attention.
He's writing the age I am now.
I want to say: you don't die for years.
He can't hear me, no more than Hector, Socrates.

I picture him casting, casting
into some high lochan
and a shadow on the opposite bank;
the delicate arcs of two mirrored lines,
the finicky business of flies,
and the two of them, still as chessmen,
each bent with all his art
on reeling the other in.

Parentheses bother me, too,
(enter a life, stage left; exit right),
as though there were beginnings
and endings. No such things.
The salmon go back into the water.

No brackets for you, MacCaig.
Still learning me your language.

---

* Pibroch: a tune played by a single piper.
A call to a gathering, a salute, a lament,
characterised by the complexity of its grace notes.

For the true naming of the world

you need one who will recognise a fish
that has swallowed a star
that fell through the vaults of the air;
one who wears a helmet or bears a sword
forged in the heart of mountains,
from metals whose names no man ever knew,
to bear a name that can not be forgot,
a name to fit in a verse to be sung at a feast;

you need one to be sent on a quest
through silent forests, stony wastes,
to a bony church and a hillside that opens
to a way that he'll walk through all the ages,
to come dumb and dazzled to the seashore
under huge lucid skies, into the wind,
to build monasteries, to illuminate gospels;
to speak to otters, spear the sea like a gannet,
to be one with wind and with seals.

Then stones and flowers might come
to know themselves. Day's-eye, comfrey,
coltsfoot, mallow, vetch, stonecrop, feverfew.
Hornblende, granite, wolfram, flint and gneiss;
valleys might come know their depths,
and becks and burns to know the purposes of rain,
and the ways of the clough and the gorge
under blood moons, hare moons, the moon
when horns are broken. Then.

In the Meantime

because that's how it is, the sparrow
flying into the meadhall, bewildered
by smoke-reek, gusts of beer-breath,
out of the wild dark and into the half-
light of embers, sweat, the steam
of fermenting rushes, and maybe
a harp and an epic that means nothing
in a language it doesn't know, this sparrow,
frantic to be out there, and maybe
it perches on a tarry roof beam, catches
a wingtip, comes up against thatch
like a moth on a curtain, and it beats
its wings, it beats its wings, it tastes
a wind with the scent of rain, the thin
smell of snow, of stars, and somehow
it's out into the turbulence of everywhere,
and who knows what happens next.

Much Possessed
for Polly Morgan: artist and taxidermist

She keeps mynah birds and fledgling sparrows
in the freezer. Knows just how feathers lie
in a wing, the small fine down of the breast,
the jewel scales of thin reptilian feet,
the pitch of muscle, all its give and stretch.

She knows about incisions, scalpels, cuts,
how skin can tear, how to tease it from the skull
like a latex glove from a surgeon's white hand;
translucent films and also oysterish flesh,
the strength of tendons, elasticicities.

She is comfortable with the smell of alcohol,
the sweetness of decay and thaw, the sharpness
of formaldehyde. She is deft with waddings,
patient re-clothings, fine stitching, the smoothing
of plumes, and the way a beak must sit, just so.

Sometimes she looks at the backs of her hands,
imagines the bones she has never seen; imagines
the spongy maze of her lungs, the ruby kidneys,
the packed grey intestinal coil, the lens of her eye;
she thinks of her plump-muscled heart.

Bounty

A shilling for a squirrel's tail,
and two free cartridges,
that day in a wood of sycamore and beech,
blue with muzzle smoke, loud with the flat
snap, the shotgun slammed-door bang.

How neat the small hands, the dark bright pip
of the eye; how accurate the chisel teeth.
But a squirrel's tail now. A wing, a point
of balance, a thing of air, a spread fan.

Taken off with claspknives, secateurs,
cashed in like tokens at a fair. Tail after tail
like the frayed ends of old washing lines.
There's no way to put back the air

that filled them like a helmet's plume;
their curl, the jauntiness. Something softer
than the soft fur of your cat's throat,
the black gloss trim on the coat of an aunt.

Imagine a squirrel without a tail.
Think of a rat.

Wren

God thought of the smallest coin
he could make, and made the Wren
to fit, neat as a thumb in a thimble,
tail cocked like a flintlock trigger.
He should have loved the Wren more
than let the boys come smashing down
the thorn, chanting, calling: Wren!
come out! come out! come out and die.

With her hairspring call, she cannot
keep silent, the Wren, full as an egg
with alarm and urgency, her voice a tattle
of fingernails on an old tin lid.

Fragile as a chalice on its thin glass stem.
Why kill a Wren and her mid-winter song?
What did she ask for but a zipwire of air,
a tangle to hide her nest, a May full of flies?

Goldcrest

unaccountably dead,
this morning being clear as gin,
rain-soaked lawns brushed to a nap
in the night, blackthorn and hornbeam
newly wired, plugged in, switched on,
and all a-buzz.

Why choose such a morning
to be dead in? November staining
windows ruby, amber, lime;
and here you are, cupped in a palm. Too perfectly
assembled, too compact ever to have flown;
a soft plump brooch; every feather trim,
unruffled, green and gold as barley in a breeze,
every bit of you pin-sharp, smart as sixpence.

There is nothing to be done. You can't stay here.
Too much of bird in you to stay indoors,
too much sharp enquiry in each small dark eye.

Whether it cared or not

hardly came into it. I cared,
if that's the word.

It's a stony track
across the watershed
where you look down on a coral shore,
the place where the bridge was,
the black slopes of Sgurr na Stri,
and the Bad Step
grown out of the chill loch.

The adder was as a different thing,
rearing up in the stones of the path
on a day of mist at the end of a year,
and a smirr of rain on the wind.
Its mouth gaped white and wide.
It stared. It stared.

Then it shut its mouth,
and its head went the shape you knew
the head of a snake should be.
Its thin tongue flickered in a way you knew
was what the tongue
of a snake should do.

Then it slid. You can't tell how
they do that, how the muscles work.
It slid into the bracken and the cold.

I don't know what to make of it.

A Dry Place

Remember
    the quickness
of the simple snake,
the brightness of his eye.

    Don't blame him,
who asks only for sun
and a dry place

Lacerta Lapida

Everywhere this lexicon of dust, a harvest
of spikes, brittle thistles, sharp burrs, and you,

  more ancient than mountains, older than the sun;
  sucked out, juiced, tunnelled by ants;

each of your four feet the hand of a five-fingered bird,
your jaw clamped in its flint arrow skull;

you're all weapon, you're elvish chain mail,
you're chips of glass, enamel, tessera;

you're flickering, you're needle quick; why don't you stitch
the warp and weft of yellow grass, faster than flies?

Why are you dry and stiff? When did you stop?
Why have we brought you these wild white flowers?

One Sunday

this narrow morning street
is shadowed canyon-cold and quiet
as an aftermath where the woman
in a shapeless cardigan tips out a bucket
and sluices granite setts as blue as mussels
and at the street's steep end the sun has warmed
the church whose doors are set with steel
and damascened with hammered copper nails
and underneath the latticed iron balcony
a corrugated iron garage door is rattled up
and no one is coming out but
three men in biker boots and leathers
as pink and lemon lycra cyclists
wind round the curve and out of sight
and an old man shuffles carefully
across the way and disappears
and the blind man slowly taps his way
along the wall and his mouth is pursed
and his smoke black glasses reflect no light
and the church bell's tolling flat and cracked
across the valley's olives wild flowers oranges
the soil as pale as pastry the million terraces
the wind-scored crumbling turrets
piercings crenellations revetements
the patchwork roofs the tiles
geraniums that want for sun
behind black iron grilles
and all the trodden paths the tumbled stone
the tended trees the ironwork on peeling doors
the blue graffiti on a Moorish wall
a cistern's cool greenness and slowly

turning into rust this car
down in the gulley where the road
turns steep and sharp back on itself
and the river long since drained into its bed
and all this myriad strange particular stuff

you turn a corner and stop short fearing to fall
into distances where mountains live
that only birds can understand
and dazed by space stare into this endlessness
beyond a narrow street
where a woman in the quiet early Sunday morning
has sluiced the granite setts
until they shine like mussel shells

Colouring in

This is what I have learned
in the streets of my town which is made of stone.

There are thirty seven steps. At the foot,
in a cold iron pot, are flowers,
soft and velvet as inside of my cat's ear.

They tell me: these are blue.
They say: the sky is blue, the last house of the street
is blue and so is Mary the Mother of God of the Miracles.

My cat's soft velvet ear is blue. The sky is soft,
also the last house, and the Mother of God.

The church is built of brick, which is rough-edged
straight-lined, sharp-angled. And this is yellow.
Yellow is the shape of bricks.

Birds clap from the tower where the bell is hung.
They sound like wet cloths on a line in a gust.
Laundry looks like birds. A line of washing
chatters and fratches. Sparrow laundry.

Pale grey is a roughness on my fingertips.
Green whispers and smells of rain.

On days like this warm day
the sky is a cat's ear
and is listening me.

First Pressing

In the Carrer de la Mare de Deu del Miracle,
he's slicked up for the camera; a clean shirt,
hair like a young Sinatra, black and oiled.
This is his olive press, this monumental thing,
the great stone drum, its drive shafts, gear train,
smoke-dark beams. Set going it will shake the street.

There's a charred chair and a black stove
belching smoke. Stains on the whitewashed walls
dark as ancient blood. You half expect a Torquemada
in the room, and not these stocky lads
in jumpers, posed judiciously about the door.
A head of steam is building, somewhere.

The mill turns quicker than you'd think,
crushing tumbled loads of olives, plump and pink,
to a slurried tapenade as thick as pebbledash;
he lingers by the big brass pressure gauge,
the multiplying power of chains of gears;
the mill goes turning, turning, balanced, huge.

The pressing, the stacked and beautifully
woven filter mats, the cast iron frame that gleams
like every other metal thing with its fine oil film,
is shown without much fuss. This is the pressing; as you see.
Equally, the slapping of successive pads, the way
the crumbling cake is shucked in skips.

The drama that attends the combed-back hair,
the narrow hips, is saved for ladling the oil;
gold sluices the bright steel funnel, falls soundlessly
into the drum. Taste it now, the virgin oil, quick, quick
before its fruit and pepper green leaf savour fades,
before he takes a bow and brings his curtain down.

Two weeks on, he tips his tractor off the bancal.
A stone course on the edge has shifted,
and he has gone too close. He's broken,
and pressed in the earth and his blood is dark
in the chalk-grey loam. The diesel coughs;
it shudders once and stops. Hot metal ticks and cools.

His new oil is barely cold in its fresh-racked jars,
packed in clean straw in the cellar, in the Street
of the Mother of God of the Miracles.

All over the city

> ... *wiseowl Leeds*
> *pro rege et lege schools, nobody needs*
> *your drills and chanting*
> —Tony Harrison: 'The Rhubarbarians'

the word goes round
there'll be a dole of bread at St Anne's gates
you want to get down there
they're making a film of
the Revelation of St John the Divine
at the library
Johnny Depp and Kate Blanchett are in it
the word goes round
they've caught the Supermarket Poisoner
they've caught him
they're bringing him up Albion Street
you want to get down there
it's right
three Virgins all in green
are dancing on the Aire
at the Armouries below the weirs
the river has gone blue a sapphire blue
salmon are leaping
no one knows what it means
all over the city the word goes round
angels have stood barefoot
on the Town Hall steps
it's right
they're walking up the Headrow
two-by-two their heads are shaved
they're all in white they're walking on thorns
the owls have flown the white towers
they're circling Milennium Square
making wild cries

and the starlings are back
the Black Prince is riding up Vicar Lane
to the Corn Exchange and thousands
are following him and singing
all over the city the word goes round
and no one knows what it means

A City of the Plain

From the top of a bus on the edge of the hills,
you felt you might fly over all the miles
of rhubarb and kale, thin commons, shabby sheep,
to the snowglobe city, its one white tower;
the golden glint of owls.

Tideline city left by the ebb
of a sea that never returned,
it grew like black coral or coalesced
from what drained off the hills
or what fell from the cloud that hung over it.

A reef of blackened brick,
all its crusted canyons loud
with starlings, the crooning
of bluntbeaked, headbutting pigeons.

City of lightless arches, handsome streets,
city of suits and sweatshops,
city of glamour and Blackshirts.

City whose river runs sluggish with rinsings,
old and grey, under iron bridges, over churning weirs.

Dark city under the stare of owls.

According to their Cloth

I knew one man made a forced march in a column,
full pack and rifle; heat and scrub, humidity, thick dust;
forty miles in a single day and never knew a battle plan.

One man who fell from a plane
in a night full of parachutes,
the wind white silk; the dark sound of planes
dwindling up into the night and him falling into fiasco;
who taught history, who clung to Communism
like a Tudor martyr to a relic.

Another who drove his jeep into something
that men might make, experimenting
in a slovenly way with making up an idea of hell;
into a camp made out of rust and rot,
of wire and sweet black smoke and rags and sweat;
No one came to liberate him;
no one to take his eyes from the dark,
no-one to bring him back from the dead.

The one I loved most spun yarn
for uniforms and army blankets.
Reserved occupation. Conchie.
All the same to him. Nobody tried to kill me.
He cut his coat according to his cloth.
Took his suit lengths into Leeds,
to Jewish tailors, emigrés
in small dark shops in narrow streets.

You don't choose where you are in history.
You cut your coat
and wear it.

Short Back and Sides

It's fine, Stan's hair. His wife, Vera, says:
'He gets it from his mother.
They were all fine haired, her side.'

He's soft-skinned, too. Big hands
with liver spots. They tremble, agitate
an invisible test tube, like a chemist.

Big ears, lobes like small ox-tongues.
He likes his hair cut short.
Curious to be holding his head still,

gentling the clippers in the back of his neck,
hearing the buzz, feeling light hairs fall.
I've eaten snake, he says. A python.

He could butcher anything the lads brought in.
He'll not eat curry. When you smell that
you know you're closing on a village.

On Recon. they'd take the headman's son.
Shackle him on the bonnet of the Jeep.
See, if no one made a fuss we'd know

no Japs was up the trail. Drive him for a bit
then let him off. The skin of his scalp is fragile,
scissors cold on the pink of the skull.

His goalkeeper's hands beat a soft
tattoo against his knee. When he remembers
he clasps them like a handshake, or a prayer.

In jungle once, he came upon a pal
pinioned to a tree, opened up from throat to groin,
his piled entrails at his feet, a black buzz of flies.

I've never told our Vera that. I tidy round his neck.
I'll shake the teatowel outside on the step,
watch the hair blow, like dandelion clocks.

His hands have freed themselves.
He has forgotten them.

What the Owls Saw

They watched with gilded eyes.

Out from the west, a flick of black sleet, spatterings,
a fattening squall like the ash of a great burning
and it fell on the city.
Sequin glints: sapphire, silver, emerald,
a great winnowing, the sieving and sifting of wings,
the glitter of a million eyes and beaks and claws
battening on every coign and corniced ledge.

The owls watched them seethe
on carved acanthus, crockets, ogees, orioles,
pediments and finials, and architraves,
scrabbling on the bronze Black Prince, fratching and clawing
and stropping beaks, crusting everything with guano
that squirmed and writhed with teeming things.
Ravenous the birds.

Night after night. Gone at first light. The owls saw them go
into big skies, over fields and woods: midge clouds,
fractals of iron filings, a distant dance.

And so it went and the owls stared down the years,
and nothing changed until it did,

the day the mazy dance grew frantic fast, spiralled madly
into itself and clenched to the size of a bee,
and, faster than light, drilled through the crust
of the world and into its turning core,
the shiver of the hot machine. Into its black fire
the starlings went, and that's where they stayed.

Because the phoenix is just a story.
Because what's burned stays burned.

The owls stared out
across a city shining white, a coral reef
of turrets, towers, splintering light

lensed like the eyes of the fly.
There was nowhere to hide. The owls went blind,
they cried for the dark. They went mad.

What the Owls Dreamed

The owls went blind;
they stared. Everything was black.
They could see
whatever they wanted.

Time breathed in. One great indrawn breath.

The drained muck of mills and foundries
shrank back up the river's long gut.
Eel and trout and salmon came after.
The river grew bright with air.
In the east, the seas sank,
Drowned ships, sailors, streets and steeples
steamed in the sun.

The reef of the city unbuilt
into forest and marsh
thick with flies, and the river
gathered itself, grew wide and turbulent,
its bunched muscles slid
and flexed under its skin;
it raced like surf up the dale,
drowning eyebright and heartsease,
scattering the stones of small towns,
the crumbled footings of farms,
and it hurled itself in a welter
up the white cliffs of Craven,
it foamed on the tessellate stone
in rainbows and mist,

drank itself under
a mile high wall of ice
that shimmered with trapped stars.

The world went silent.

The owls stared and stared. It was white.
There were no kings. No laws.
The owls froze. Their hearts stopped.

A Proper Job

There's more to this than people think.
So listen. See, you want to get the build-up right.
That one I took you to last week. All wrong.
What's the good of flogging a chap
till he can't carry the thing? He only ends up
dropping it, spectators want to help,
military jump in. A bloody circus.

Take my advice. You want to keep them
fit and fed and fresh. They'll not thank you,
but just think on. You're not there to cheer them up.
Just to do a proper job.

Make sure you order oak
that's been let to lie a year or two.
You need to cut a solid six by six,
one tight lap joint, nice and snug.
Four clean dowels, olive;
don't get palmed off with pine ...
If it does get dropped you don't want
that cross-piece twisting.
Causes too much bother later on.

Nails? Get them from that blacksmith
by the market. You'll want clean-cut, well tapered,
a good nine inch.
Plan to use just the three, but get six.
They can break if you don't catch them right,
and anyway a big lad might need
a couple in each wrist

I'll tell you all about the way

to lie them down, the knots,
the bones to get between,
the hoisting and the dropping in the slot
when we've had our snap.

But just one thing. You get it right.
You don't want another carry on
like the one last week.
The one it turned out wasn't dead.
Never hear the last of that

A Dreadful Trade

You need a head for heights ... that's true.
I like the samphire gathering. Born to it.
Out on the cliffside with the lad. No wind.
A new rope, well-wetted, clean and firmly set.

Gulls and their fluster and noise
as we come down the chalk, small stones
and flakes fluttering off into space,
white birds jostling off on the updraught.

Dark green samphire clustered. A nice day.
One to take your time, hang like a bird,
listen to the sea talking, the blind man
and his boy on the very edge, talking back.

And here's a thing. Rattle and chink of flint
and shingle. A line of men in mail, all glitter,
and one in gold, dressed like you think a king
should dress. The sea took away the words.

Then he walks into the sea, all in gold,
his cloak swirls in the breaking waves,
and he holds up his arms and shouts at the sea.
The sea just keeps coming in. He stands there

till it reaches near his chest. Then he wades out,
wrings the brine from his cloak, and everyone
kneels down, and they hang their heads.
Then they all went off. I've often wondered

what it was all about. Still. 'Time and tide'.
All that. You can't hang about. Mouths to feed.
We stuffed our bags. No one fell off. On the way
up we got gulls' eggs. Yes ... a right good day.

A Cunning Woman

It starts with goats.
I can find a lost kid.
I can talk a tangled ram from a thicket.

Or it starts with weather.
I can smell a coming on of rain, I can scry a cloud.
Or with childbed.
I can hold a hand and cool a brow,
tie a navelstring. About blood I have no feelings.
I can clean and reddle up. Infuse a herb.

Or it starts with flowers. I know their names:
Eyebright; Penny Royal; Ragged Robin; Dodder.
It starts with words.
I believe there is no-one knows I can read.

I have no illusions. My skin is clear.
My hair is rinsed, my breath sweet.
I chew camomile and mint.
My eyes have no guile; I have studied them
in a pewter basin of clear springwater.

It starts with not fearing the dead
who have no need for water or clean linen,
but I wash them still and make them neat.

It ends in water and weed and silt.
It ends in pitch and blister, the spit of fat and fire.
One way. Or another.

Myra

You look at me and I know
what you think
you think that I know
where the dead are buried.
and I tell you what
I dream
I dream of cottongrass
its million white heads
its tender flowers
streaming white
like the blood of Jesus
like the love and mercy of Jesus
white as forgiveness
white as the rainy wind
and there are no bodies
if there ever were
bones sunk in the peat
its weeping black dams
they are gone in the whin
in the bracken
ground small
between millstones
and you think I know
where the bodies are buried
but I know I can look
in this mirror of steel
and I do not know for a second
the woman who stares back at me

Winnie

You dream of cottongrass
of threaded ghosts of baby's hair,
white water spilled on blackstone grit.

You know that you will never know
where your boy is, has been
this forty year and more;

you know this as you know
the iron and salt of hot rare meat
the smell of his skull, his skin.

Thin winds pick among the rags
and bones of brittle heather,
sunken jaggers' roads;

trouble dammed black waters,
the sour weeping of turned turfs
that won't give up what's held

where men in raincoats walk
in ragged lines with long white rods
testing the depth and smell

of the peat the way a shepherd
probes drifted Pennine snow
for buried sheep that eat their own fleece.

You knew such things could be,
breathed vowels. Air.

Now you know nothing else –

the texture of a house
this pale moth-knowing
in a shadowed room,

ringed by black moors, dark humps:
tumbled cairns that mock
the lost, that will not show the way

Banked up

brittle as a mirror
worrying at little lines
exquisite as ants or wasps
half-aware of an open window
banging somewhere in this long dark house
in a clenched valley
of cold chimneys and black walls
cemented with orphans' bones
of trees flogging themselves to death
balsam flattened by the weight of air
she cramps herself small and smaller
dreams of dwindling
into the fastness of a shell
white under a full moon
in a sky of no wind

somewhere out in the yard a bucket has blown over
rackets about the cobbles like a big man in a rage
like a man who'd smash his fist into a gritstone wall
and sing about the blood

Lutenist

Twenty four taut strings to tune
to odd diminished minor keys,
he fingers three-hundred-year-old
ghosts of runs and chords, spins
thin and melancholy tunes
to mesh the shades of courtiers
who dream of intrigue, poisonings,
of powdered courtesans, corrupt
fops with mercury-blackened teeth,
the whimperings of Berwick witches,
the smell and reek of their burning;
the wet whisper of a flenser's blade,
amber oil brimming the huge cask
of a blue whale's head; the white
shadows of a hunting owl;
a room of phantoms, minor chords.

Chimes

He hopes that tenor has been put to rights,
that the sound box will ring true.
He grasps the new tail-end
and takes a steady pull, feels for
resistance, up there in the headstock,
for its poise, its balance, and wonders
if tonight there'll be no odd-struck bell,
no coming late-of-hand.

He has in mind a ring
of shining points
each coming in precisely
like waves come to the shore
then sliding back into themselves,
breaking from the louvred tower
till all the valley's mills,
and all the forges and the cooling towers
of the plains beyond
are brim-full of God.

Cold Comfort

You forget parties
spent behind a sofa
in a room so thick with smoke
you couldn't see the sofa,
when you were one of the ones without a girl

the way you made do
with being thin and wearing black
and James-Dean-squinting through the smoke.
Enigmatic dark and tragic
except that it was Orbison, except that it was
Only the Lonely, except that it was
When will I be loved,

but anyway, one Christmas night
behind a sofa and the girl you thought you'd brought
is somewhere else with someone else
in the swirly jazz-club smoke you picture
in your all-in-black and you really
love her because that's what you do
and that's what I did, then,

which is why when she said
that someone else had gone
and would I walk her home
then that's what I did
because that's what I did, then,

and I knew it was four miles
and all up hill and hard snow underfoot

and air that hurt to breathe
and after all she held my hand

and I don't remember a single thing we said
and the frost was brilliant
and I never even kissed her

and I didn't even feel resentful
but walked the four miles home
and the fields at the top were glittery as glee
and the light turned up on its head
and the sky was orange-blue like the nimbus of a moon

there wasn't a sound

there wasn't a wind
there wasn't a car
the street lights were out

I think I have never been so cold

St Ives/Porthmeor 1953

Backs to the sea-wall sail-lofts, the gas-works' bulk,
its rusting iron work shuts out the town.
Squint into a dazzle of gemstone blue,
a bright scoop fringed with lacy white,
and out, beyond, a current's dark rip.

Sunday on the sands with Charlie Stevens, his day off
from bakehouse fire and floury air, from harbour gulls,
the smell of fish. Charlie and his family. Nieces, nephews,
his married sons, and his youngest daughter's chap
– policeman, lifeguard, loose-forward for Redruth –
who says to me: I'll take you for a proper swim.

You take proper care of him now, Edward, Charlie says.

He takes me out a quarter of a mile or more.
He says. Look. Up, behind, beyond the sea wall's
a teetering graveyard, a shutter of slate roofs,
moor edge, sky. Pale sand is sprinkled like a cake
with small dots of colour. My family. Charlie's family.

Outside the headlands' circling arms.
the weight of sea is pulling like the moon. I cannot
feel my feet in the silky cold. Edward says: wave.

This much

I remember:
the small neat creases, the crook of each elbow,
the crook of each knee, the soft place
between your neck and your shoulder,
and the tight whorls of dark hair
tattooing your skull, and the delight,
the wide pink of your open mouth
as you came shedding light and bright water
out of your bath, how you sank
in the fleece of a fat white towel,
and you lay on your back on her knee
and you danced,
how you pedalled and trod on the air,
and how pale the soles of your feet.
You were mangoes, grapes, you were apricots,
all your round warm limbs, your eyes.
How your name made you smile;
how we said it over and over, your name;
how we wanted to make that smile.
And I remember
how we would take you away,
why your name could not come too,
why we must leave it behind,
how we feared for your smile.

I made this box,

ran quick lead in the veins of driftwood roots,
the silver grain of bleached board and the wind-eyes
of burnished beachstones – rose quartz, granite, flint,
bound them with silver wire to honey oak, red pine,
and clenched them tight with sea-rust iron nails.

I made this box for you

I filled it with fragments, beachcombed
sea glass, wisps of snagged wool.
I wanted you to know
the random loveliness of being alive,
to know it in your bones and blood.

I put in:

snow, to remember draughts
and rooms with cold corners;

a black handled knife, sharp as silk
in a grey-vaulted market, the scent

of cut flowers to show that fathers
give like the gods; a bicycle stammering

through stems of barley, willowherb,
to understand that gravity may be defied;

the humped glass of a brown river,
black branches snagged on the weir's rim;

these bundled letters in different hands
and inks to show how words fall short of love.

I put in riddles:
silhouettes of mountains, oiled gun barrels,
a sheriff's badge, a dust-blown street,

a child running in a drift of grasses,
a scrubbed deal table in a pitman's house.

I wondered if you'd find the answers
or if I might understand the questions.

I did not want to put inside my box
your cold clay mouth
this pale oak chamfered cube
and my two hands holding it, all

I wanted was you holding my box
in a high place
where you could only fly, not fall

It was a morning like this

a Sunday morning. The sun shone.
It was July. It was a morning like this,
your ex-wife at the back door,
and why would she tell you
your son was dead, or had died,
or had been in an accident
on a morning like this still
not fully woken, a morning of sun
to drive into Chapeltown to drive
to a police station that's called
The Old Police Station now, that's
a bijou gastropub but then was just
a police station full of Sunday morning
sadness, and a morning something
like this and two young coppers
who thought we'd need somewhere
quiet at the back which turned out
to smell of smoke, that had a pool table
and coffee rings, and no-one knew
how to start or what to ask but
it was a morning much like this
they asked if we knew a tower block
behind the Merrion Centre or if
we had a connection to a tower block
and a ring with a skull and a brown
leather case and did we know if
our son had friends in a tower block
behind the Merrion Centre and
we might as well have been asked
about tree rings or chaos theory

or fractals on a July morning and
one young copper saying that
he didn't think it made sense
for cannabis to be illegal and
what harm did it do really and
how it wasted everybody's time
and I don't know why I'd remember
that except it was a morning like this
I learned what waste might mean.

A Weak Force

there's sometimes a loss you can't imagine;
the lives never lived by your children, or
by the one who simply stopped
in the time it takes
to fall to the ground
from the top of a tower block.

They say gravity is a weak force.
I say the moon will tug a trillion tons
of salt sea from its shore.
I say a mountain range will pull a snowmelt
puddle out of shape.
I say gravity can draw a boy
through a window
and into the air.

There is loss no one can imagine.

In the no time between
falling and not falling
you learned the art of not falling;

beneath you burned
the lights of Sheepscar, Harehills,
Briggate, Vicar Lane;
lights shone in the glass arcades,
on the tiles, on the gantries of tall cranes;
motorway tail lights trailed ribbons of red,
and you were far beyond falling.

Because you shut your eyes
because you always shut your eyes
you closed them tight as cockleshells
because when you did that the world

would go away the world
would not see you.

I remember how you ran like a dream.
I remember how you laughed when I swore
I would catch you.

Then you flared you went out
you flared like a moth and you blew
away over the lights over the canal
the river the sour moors the cottongrass
the mills of the plain
and over the sea and over the sea
and the bright west
and you sank like the sun.

Above all: Mallory on Everest

How did we get here, starved of air
in a skitter of blown ice,
in the dazzle, in a rare thin sky?

If I could, I'd kneel, I'd want
to touch the wind-cured vellum
of your shoulder, to trace
the tent of your ribs,
the sharp jut of your jaw,
your dry empty eyes.

I'd want to gather up
your scattered threads,
parched wallet, buttons,
and I'd like to tell you
that I can't forgive you;
not for the way you chose
cold and altitude,
for the way you would love
this death more than children, wife.

When I think of this I cannot think
however I might come down.

Untrammelled

High on the shoulder of Everest
Mallory, Irving, Somerville, Odell
are reading 'Kubla Khan',
a sunny pleasure dome with caves of ice.
It is beyond cold. Their fingers grow white.

How much stuff they took, the British
in the Himalaya. Other people carried it.
And animals. Ponies, oxen, yak.
Small men impossibly burdened
with crates as big as bungalows,

hauling stuff through steamy scrub,
the emery wind of gravel deserts,
slovenly moraines and rotten snow
yellow as bad teeth, under the blue
glamour, the opalescence of seracs,

across blinding snowfields, below
golden cliffs and corniced ridges,
the streaming prayer flags of spindrift
crystals, and always up and up
and into a thinner air.

Mallory pens a letter
that will reach his Ruth, with others,
months after he has died.
This is their mountain.
This is their time. Their eyes are full
of the highest places under heaven.

Unhampered by its gravity they unpack
a Fortnums hamper and dine
on quails in paté, and fine champagne,
a 1915 Montebello.

Then, untrammelled, they walk on
and up, into infinity.

Falling apart

They're softly lit, and young and full of love
and incredulity; Ruth's hair is a nimbus.
It seems they share their love like a single skin;
he remembers how it feels, he tells her, in the letters
that he writes in tents half-buried under spindrift snow,
before he walks off a corniced ridge, before a fall

out of airless height, and into mystery, a fall
from grace, and from his Ruth, helpless with love,
who he leaves again and again, while his letters
promise, over and over, there'll be no more cloud
to come between them, no more ice to chill their skin;
those letters that always seem to smell of snow –

glamorous and exotic, she thinks – of snow,
and not of him – climbing always, into clouds,
the midden-snouts of glaciers, many-lettered
prayer flags unthreading in dry winds that skin
golden walls to a sheen, the height he loves
and fears, and the gulf he will have to fall

through, spiralling down years and years, falling
further than history; she has only his letters
that keep arriving though he's dead, full of his love
and the snow that filled his eyes. Stripped to his skin
he'll lie for years, ageless, white, beautiful as snow.
She grows old. His children grow old. He mists

in their minds, milky as cataracts, and clouds
come on and on, building and unbuilding snow
in thin winds that patiently unpick their love,
snipping each frayed thread, scattering his letters,
his painfully inked words; sepia leaves, they fall

into silence, and he shrinks into his shroud of skin,
and small crystals fill his eyes, and his skin
is ivory as altitude, white as new snow;
he sets into his own sepulchre; his fall
is a fall into speechlessness and separation. Love
is something he's too old to learn. His letters say
Ruth I love you. His love was in summit cloud.

It was stone enchanted him. Cold altitude, and snow.
Cirrus had all his love. He forgot how soft was her skin.
His fingers frosted white, he could never hold her, always let her fall.

George Mallory, Everest pioneer. d.June 1924.
leaving his wife, Ruth, and three young children

Seen from Above

That time, belayed high up on Gimmer Crag
we watched a tiny Mini puttering
up the Langdale road. Maybe, watching
minute climbers on the cliff he missed
the sharp left turn, and, with a tinkling
of stone, ran slap into the boundary wall.
There was a little plume of steam.
We smiled. Above us in the quiet
a kestrel hovered; sheep called and cropped.

Distance takes away all difficulty.
One clear morning, seen from the corrie rim,
the dubious track, the awkward scree,
the bogs, the ankle-turning boulder-field
resolved themselves into a pleasing
textured fabric: acid-greens and amber,
russets, and cool greys. Rocks as big as buses
shrank to a spill of sugar, picnic crumbs.

Flying gives assurance that your maps are true.
Halfway up England, once, clouds parted;
there below, the Dark Peak's pewter lakes,
cooling-tower cruet sets, cat's cradle
rivers, motorways, and suddenly, my street.
My house. I could see my car. Absurdly pleased,
to have this mile high view that proved
that Google Earth, and where I live, is real.

Everything is simpler from above –
the way the earth explains itself,
why a river runs the way it does. Why
gods look down from mountaintops,
and heaven is forever in the sky.

When the keel grated

we paid it not much heed.
it would happen, now and then.

But it groaned, and there was splintering
and a lurch when everything pitched sideways.

We waited for the boat to right itself,
all the 'tween decks a slurry of shit and hay,
and tusks and wings and fur and legs
and scales and beaks. Bedlam.

It stayed canted.
Not easy to get up on top,
but the view was staggering.
Waters streaming into boiling gullies,
geysers, great silver gouts and belches,
and everywhere stinking. Mud, gravel,
pebbles, dead men bloating, black clots of leaf,
gasping fish. The sun. So huge. And white.
Steam.

Animals got themselves out, fighting, rutting.
Some fell down waterfalls. Some stuck in mud
or sank and suffocated. What could we do?
We did wonder at the arch
in the sky. All those colours.

Maybe we should have prayed.
Or tried to light a fire.

We were past caring.
Just glad to be off that boat,
to follow the ebb, down.
And not look back.

The Fisherman's Church of Talmont-sur-Gironde

When faith was a given thing,
like hunger and child mortality,
masses were sung here for an English king.

The churches of the Charente sit like chessmen
on the plain, but this one just grows
out of the cliff, where the river ends.

It touches the sky, like leaves. It holds
space as easily as water in a glass,
high above the tides, the dark shoals.

Inside is white, as quiet as prayers,
as ghosts of Ave Marias, candle smoke.
Sparrows fly in the windless tower.

I have no faith, but feel the balm
of others' faith in this white, quiet place.
Light a candle for its small flame.

Curtain call

a day of fasting, a day
of constant intervention, of no rest,
a day of tests, the taking of blood,
the comfortable squeeze of a pressure cuff,
a day of ones who stand beside you silently
and write notes, and you think,
because you've worked in warehouses,
you're being stockchecked,
and nurses say brightly: scratch,
the ones who know the mysteries of pain,
all about it, pain they never feel,
who digitise it, ask you on a scale of one to ten
to rate your misery, and rhapsodise
on paracetamol; the trim girls
with wide blue belts and flat-soled shoes,
who carefully push hollow needles into
the thin skin on the back of your hand and neatly
tape them down,
and the suntanned breezy men, anaesthetists
who talk at length incomprehensibly and go,
and all around, the extras,
lighting crew and hangers-on,
who idly watch you being made up and dressed
while you fail to remember any lines for this part
that you've never played
because before you know
it's curtain up, you're centre stage,
and everybody staring.

Then the lights go off.

30 years
of smith|doorstop poets

Moniza Alvi, David Annwn, Simon Armitage, Jane Aspinall, Ann Atkinson, David Attwooll, Anne-Marie Austin, Sally Baker, Mike Barlow, Kate Bass, Paul Batchelor, Suzanne Batty, Zeina Hashem Beck, Chris Beckett, Peter Bennet, Catherine Benson, Gerard Benson, Paul Bentley, Sujata Bhatt, David Borrott, Nina Boyd, Maxwell Boyle, Sue Boyle, Carol Brierly, Susan Bright, Carole Bromley, Sue Butler, Peter Carpenter, James Caruth, Liz Cashdan, Dennis Casling, Julia Casterton, Claire Chapman, Debjani Chatterjee, Linda Chase, Geraldine Clarkson, Stephanie Conn, Stanley Cook, Bob Cooper, Jennifer Copley, Julia Copus, Rosaleen Croghan, Tim Cumming, Paula Cunningham, Simon Currie, Duncan Curry, Ann Dancy, Emma Danes, Peter Daniels, Peter Daniels Luczinski, Joyce Darke, Jonathan Davidson, Kwame Dawes, Owen Davis, Julia Deakin, Nichola Deane, Steve Dearden, Patricia Debney, Mike DiPlacido, Maura Dooley, Tim Dooley, Jane Draycott, Basil du Toit, Christy Ducker, Carol Ann Duffy, Sue Dymoke, Stephen Duncan, Suzannah Evans, Michael Farley, Rebecca Farmer, Nell Farrell, Catherine Fisher, Janet Fisher, Anna Fissler, Andrew Forster, Katherine Frost, Sam Gardiner, Adele Gèras, Sally Goldsmith, Yvonne Green, David Grubb, Harry Guest, Robert Hamberger, David Harmer, Sophie Hannah, John Harvey, Jo Haslam, Geoff Hattersley, Jeanette Hattersley, Selima Hill, John Hilton, Andrea Holland, Holly Hopkins, Sian Hughes, Keith Jafrate, Lesley Jefferies, Chris Jones, Mimi Khalvati, John Killick, Jenny King, Mary King, Stephen Knight, Judith Lal, John Lancaster, Peter Lane, Michael Laskey, Kim Lasky, Brenda Lealman, Tim Liardet, Katherine Lightfoot, Semyon Izrailevich Lipkin, John Lyons, Maitreyabandhu, Paul Matthews, Eleanor Maxted, John McAuliffe, Michael McCarthy, Rachel McCarthy, Patrick McGuinness, Kath McKay, Paul McLoughlin, Hugh McMillan, Ian McMillan, Allison McVety, Julie Mellor, Hilary Menos, Paul Mills, Hubert Moore, Kim Moore, David Morley, Sarah Morris, Blake Morrison, Paul Munden, Daljit Nagra, Dorothy Nimmo, Stephanie Norgate, Christopher North, Carita Nystrom, Sean O'Brien, Padraig O'Morain, Mark Pajak, Nigel Pantling, Alan Payne, Pascale Petit, Stuart Pickford, Ann Pilling, Jim Pollard, Wayne Price, Simon Rae, Irene Rawnsley, Ed Reiss, Neil Roberts, Marlynn Rosario, Padraig Rooney, Jane Routh, Peter Sansom, Tom Sastry, Michael Schmidt, Myra Schneider, Rosie Shepperd, Lemn Sissay, Felicity Skelton, Catherine Smith, Elspeth Smith, Joan Jobe Smith, Cherry Smyth, Martin Stannard, Pauline Stainer, Paul Stephenson, Mandy Sutter, Matthew Sweeney, Diana Syder, David Tait, Pam Thompson, Dennis Travis, Susan Utting, Stephen Waling, Martin Wiley, Tony Williams, Ben Wilkinson, Andrew Wilson, David Wilson, River Wolton, Sue Wood, Anna Woodford, Cliff Yates, Luke Samuel Yates

Laureate's Choice 2015 pamphlets
still available from the Poetry Business

David Borrott | Nichola Deane | Rachel McCarthy | Wayne Price

This is a varied but coherent collection, tender, imaginative and clear-eyed. – Carol Ann Duffy

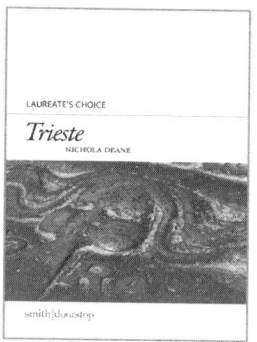

A poet both sophisticated and lyrically charged who deploys imagery that is both precise and daring. – Carol Ann Duffy

Here are bold poems in a collection that is much more than the sum of its mesmerising parts.
– Carol Ann Duffy

A remarkable new poet who is intelligent, insightful, imaginative and utterly assured.
– Carol Ann Duffy

£7.50 each or all 4 for £20
www.poetrybusiness.co.uk